MEDICINE

AND

THE SAME

MEDICINE

AND

THE SAME

TWO PLAYS BY

ENDA WALSH

THEATRE COMMUNICATIONS GROUP
NEW YORK
2021

Medicine and *The Same* is published by Theatre Communications Group, Inc.,
520 Eighth Avenue, 24th Floor, New York, NY 10018-4156

This volume is published in arrangement with Nick Hern Books Limited,
The Glasshouse, 49a Goldhawk Road, London, W12 8QP

This publication is made possible in part by the New York State Council on the
Arts with the support of Governor's office and the New York State Legislature.

TCG books are exclusively distributed to the book trade by
Consortium Book Sales and Distribution.

A catalogue record for this book is available from the Library of Congress.

ISBN 978-1-63670-096-0 (paperback)

Cover design by Lisa Govan

Cover image: Domhnall Gleeson, photograph by Alex Sapienza,
courtesy of Landmark Productions

First TCG Edition, November 2021

CONTENTS

MEDICINE

Medicine received its world premiere at the Traverse Theatre as part of Edinburgh International Festival on August 7, 2021, prior to its opening at the Galway International Arts Festival on September 4, 2021. It was developed with the support of the National Theatre, London. Produced by Landmark Productions and Galway International Arts Festival, it was subsequently produced at St. Anne's Warehouse in Brooklyn. The cast included:

John	Domhnall Gleeson
Mary 1	Aoife Duffin
Mary 2	Clare Barrett
Drummer	Seán Carpio

Director   Enda Walsh
Composer   Teho Teardo
Designer   Jamie Vartan
Lighting Designer   Adam Silverman
Sound Designer   Helen Atkinson
Costume Designer   Joan O'Clery
Live Drumming   Seán Carpio
(Composition and performance)

CHARACTERS

JOHN KANE
OLD MAN/MARY 1
LOBSTER/MARY 2

Also a DRUMMER, *and recorded voices*

This text went to press before the end of rehearsals and so may differ slightly from the play as performed.

A curtain opens as fluorescent lights flicker on – and JOHN KANE *is walking into this room – and away from a door that's closing on the back wall.*

Outside the room – we can hear clearly the sound of the institution – in the distance people shouting and calling – doors banging, a faraway television...

The room looks like it's used for various activities like table tennis and bingo and badminton.

There's a banner overhead reading 'Congratulations' – and some tired balloons and a trestle table with the remains of some party food and soft drinks.

There's a table and chair, with a microphone and desk lamp on the table. Also on the table there's a battery-powered pencil sharpener, two pencils and two scripts.

Near this table – there's a full drum kit.

Just above the fluorescent lights – there's a busy lighting rig.

Visible also is a metal trolley with electronic sound equipment on it.

At the back of the room is a large booth with a glass window – were it not for the closed curtain we'd be able to see into this booth.

Stage-right – there's a much smaller booth – a cubicle, really.

JOHN *is standing in blue pyjamas and wearing beaten-up runners.*

He's holding other clothes – neatly folded.

He stares up at the 'Congratulations' banner.

He walks quickly to a bench in the far stage-left – places down his clothes and shoes – grabs a chair – and positions the chair beneath the banner and stands up to take it down –

The fluorescent lights immediately go out – but for the light in the 'cubicle'.

It's calling him. A little red light has come on – on the side of the cubicle.

JOHN *gets off the chair – walks towards the cubicle and steps inside – closes the curtain behind him – sits down at a tiny desk – putting on a pair of headphones.*

Immediately the sounds of the institution cut.

JOHN *leaning into the microphone –*

JOHN. Hello, can you hear me?

> *A long pause in which we (and* JOHN*) can hear a breath.*

I can hear you breathing…

INTERVIEWER (*voice-over*). How are you today…?

JOHN. Good. I wanted to ask what the room was used for last night. It's messy and I don't want to use up any of my time having to clean it. It smells and there's a banner hanging –

INTERVIEWER (*voice-over*). How are you today, John?

JOHN. Well, nervous! – which you can hear… I realise that the staff have to let loose now and again – but only once a year I get the opportunity to come to this room…

INTERVIEWER (*voice-over*). How are you today, John?

JOHN. I'm fine, thank you. I'm…

INTERVIEWER (*voice-over*). How long have you been in here?

> JOHN *is then heard in voiceover.*

JOHN (*voice-over*). I don't know.

INTERVIEWER (*voice-over*). And what brought you here?

JOHN (*voice-over*). That's difficult to answer.

> JOHN *sits listening to the interview.*

INTERVIEWER (*voice-over*). And whose idea was it that you'd come here, John?

JOHN (*voice-over*). My parents and a doctor in my town.

INTERVIEWER (*voice-over*). And what happened that ended up with you being here?

Suddenly the door in the back wall crashes open – an OLD MAN *is seen entering the room fast, carrying a sports bag – the door closing behind him.*

JOHN *carries on talking to the interviewer – a conversation we can't hear.*

A phone starts ringing – its ringtone is the 'By The Seaside' ringtone on the iPhone – the OLD MAN *fumbling in his jacket.*

Answering his phone –

OLD MAN. I'm late – I'm sorry – it was the bus! (*Slight pause.*) I'm not late? (*Slight pause.*) Well it seems to be the right place. (*Slight pause.*) Okay.

The call finishes.

The curtain on the large booth swiftly opens.

Through its window – in a strange green light – we and the OLD MAN *can see an enormous* LOBSTER *pouring themselves some soup from a flask.*

That's difficult to do with claws.

The OLD MAN *looks over to the cubicle as* JOHN *continues to talk to the interviewer.*

The OLD MAN *has got a little 'me time'.*

He finds a lead and attaches his phone to the sound equipment on the trolley.

He looks for a song on his phone.

The LOBSTER *removes its head and we see that it's a young woman. She drinks her soup.*

The OLD MAN *finds the song and presses play.*

Dan Hartman's 'Instant Replay' (the single version) comes on – and Dan's countdown is heard from 'Ten, nine, eight...' – it cuts the slow quiet music that was playing.

The OLD MAN*'s moustache hair has been annoying him.*

He holds his moustache.

He needs to do this quick.

He rips the moustache off his face as the countdown ends – it hurts –

OLD MAN. AAAAAAAAAAAAAHHHHHHHHHHHHHHH.

He tears off his hair (wig) and throws it on the floor – stamps on it.

This is when we recognise that 'he' is a 'she' – another young woman.

This is MARY.

As the vocal kicks in – from the sound trolley – MARY *picks up a bottle of Lucozade, opens it – thinks about drinking it.*

Drinks it. Hates it. Spits it out.

She still has OLD MAN*'s bushy eyebrows that need removing.*

The right eyebrow peels off easily.

She goes at the left eyebrow but it is stuck. Fuck.

She has an idea. Maybe liquid will help.

She pours Lucozade over her eyebrow.

It pours into and stings her eye.

MARY. FUCKING LUCOZADE!

JOHN *briefly turns towards the noise – but then turns back – continuing his conversation with the interviewer.*

MARY *drops to her knees and with two hands she wrestles with the eyebrow.*

The first chorus kicks in.

She finds some pliers on the sound trolley and tries to pull off the eyebrow with the pliers –

MARY. Fuck! Little fucker! Fuck! Fuck! Die! Die! Die!… (*Etc.*)

The eyebrow won't budge.

The third verse begins.

MARY *flings away the pliers.*

The fluorescent lights flicker back on overhead.

The YOUNG WOMAN DRESSED AS A LOBSTER *remains in the booth – flicking through* IMAGE *magazine – again the claws are a problem.*

MARY *quickly undresses out of her old-man costume – stumbling over like a child. Her runners remain on her feet.*

In her knickers and vest she crawls (commando-style), rifles through her sports bag and puts on a Les Misérables *musical T-shirt and a skirt.*

The second chorus kicks in.

She opens the booth side door – and throws in the old-man costume.

At this exact time – the LOBSTER *holds her* IMAGE *magazine up closer to her face.*

MARY *walks/shimmies over to the small table with the microphone on it. Looks down on the scripts.*

At 2.17 – MARY *sits down and checks the microphone – tapping it loudly.*

MARY (*into the mic*). That is really really interesting, John Kane. What an extraordinary deposition… let me just talk to my colleagues…

MARY *leaves the table with her script – and goes back to the sound equipment and checks a few of her audio files – lowering the volume on the third chorus of 'Instant Replay'.*

FATHER McMAHON (*voice-over, from the pulpit*). G'morning, everyone.

CONGREGATION (*voice-over*). Morning, Father.

MARY flicks through her script.

Other voices are played.

DAD (*voice-over*). What happened to John, Margaret?

MOTHER (*voice-over*). He's a stupid child – a stupid child!

Another voice.

PHILIP (*voice-over*). Do it, John – don't be a fucking idiot – take your clothes off!

Another voice.

LIAM (*voice-over*). You know what happens to cheeky people – what I have to do?

The LOBSTER finally finishes her IMAGE magazine (there's not much in it) and suddenly sees MARY in the large space. SHOCK!

At 2.54 – MARY raises the volume on 'Instant Replay'.

The LOBSTER quickly leaves the booth.

As she does a colossal wind comes from the booth.

It blows the LOBSTER over and onto the ground.

The LOBSTER crawls on the ground (commando-style) towards the door – and has to work incredibly hard at closing the booth door shut.

When she does manage it – the light in the booth goes off.

MARY turns and sees the LOBSTER.

The LOBSTER gestures to MARY to turn off the music.

MARY turns off the song.

Their exchange is fast – the LOBSTER trying to gain control –

LOBSTER. Are you the sound operator?

MARY. Yeah and actor.

LOBSTER. Secondary actor. I don't like to touch the, em...?

MARY. Sound equipment.

LOBSTER. Right. Is that John Kane in there?

MARY. Yeah he's being prepped.

LOBSTER. You've had a look at his script?

MARY. I read the synopsis on the bus – it's pretty standard.

LOBSTER. The language's a little inflated.

MARY. Yeah I saw.

LOBSTER. There's nothing we can do about that.

MARY. Any edits?

LOBSTER. Definitely – I've got a children's party at three o'clock.

MARY. Congratulations.

LOBSTER. What about the sound cues?

MARY. They're in the system.

LOBSTER. What about the drummer?

MARY. He texted me to say his bus was late.

LOBSTER. Bloody musicians.

MARY. Yeah typical.

LOBSTER. So what's with the balloons and snacks?

MARY. A staff party, I think.

LOBSTER. It smells of sick and MiWadi.

MARY. That's what counts for fun around here. Why are you dressed like a crab?

LOBSTER. I'm a lobster.

MARY. Why are you dressed like a lobster?

LOBSTER. I don't want to talk about it – it might come across as arrogance.

MARY. For the children's party?

LOBSTER. Yeah. It's themed.

MARY. *The Little Mermaid*?

LOBSTER. Exactly.

MARY. Wasn't Sebastian a crab?

The LOBSTER *thinks for a second.*

LOBSTER (*to herself*). Fuck.

Then back to MARY –

What's the first rule of acting?

MARY. Wear comfortable shoes.

LOBSTER. 'Be important.'

MARY. Okay.

LOBSTER. What we're about to do here matters.

MARY. I know that.

LOBSTER. It matters because the world is a very confusing place to live in right now and people like us – musical-theatre people – we can bring not just light enlightenment but intellectual sense – some clarity and purpose. What's with the one eyebrow?

MARY. I came from another job.

LOBSTER. And?

MARY. I can't get it off my face – it's stuck completely – it's a pain in the fucking hole.

LOBSTER. White spirit?

MARY. We've only got Lucozade.

LOBSTER. Delicious – though not a very effective acetone.

MARY. Yeah I know.

LOBSTER. We'll deal with it later. What's your name, by the way?

MARY. Mary.

LOBSTER. Mary?

MARY. Yeah.

LOBSTER. No it's not.

MARY. Yes it is.

LOBSTER. Mary's my name.

MARY. It's also my name.

MARY 2. Why don't you change your name for the purposes of our interaction?

MARY. I don't want to do that.

MARY 2. Maybe you'll find another name that suits you better.

MARY. Why don't you change your name?

MARY 2 *doesn't like her.*

MARY 2 *begins to do her voice exercises – a little too closely to* MARY*'s face.*

She then does some physical stretches and jerks to accompany the voice exercises.

She might as well be doing her own haka.

JOHN *steps out of the cubicle –* MARY *sees him.*

Hi.

JOHN. Are you the actors?

Mid-haka – MARY 2 *spins around and sees him.*

Slight pause.

A phone suddenly rings – its ringtone is a rudimentary version of 'Wilkommen' from the musical Cabaret *–*

It's MARY 2*'s phone.*

She can't get her claws into her pocket to answer it.

MARY 2 (*to* MARY). Sorry, could you…

MARY reaches into MARY 2*'s pocket – answers her phone and places the phone to* MARY 2*'s ear.*

Hello? (*Pause.*) Yes. We've just met.

JOHN *walks over to the bench in the stage-left.*

Yeah we're ready.

The call ends and MARY *places the phone back into* MARY 2*'s pocket.*

The DRUMMER *enters through the back door and into the room and goes to prepare his kit.*

MARY 2 *looks at* MARY.

Let's go!

MARY *claps her hands –*

Blackout.

A light fades up on JOHN *sitting on the bench.*

The desk lamp on the small table switches on and MARY 2 *is seated behind it taking her claws off.*

She places a pencil into the battery-powered sharpener and sharpens it.

The sharpener's ridiculously noisy – especially when amplified by the microphone.

She leans in and talks into the microphone.

Hello, John. John Kane.

JOHN. Hi.

MARY 2. Excellent pyjamas.

JOHN. Thank you – I didn't get a chance to change but I've got some more clothes...

MARY 2. Are they cotton pyjamas?

JOHN. Eh? Yes... yes I think so.

MARY 2. Right, interesting.

JOHN. Does that matter?

MARY 2 *makes a note* –

MARY 2. He is not sure... if pyjamas are cotton or not.

MARY *is placing a radio-mic on* JOHN.

JOHN. We've never talked before, me and you?

MARY 2. No never.

JOHN. Okay good.

MARY 2. You haven't forgotten me if that's what you were worried about. You were a little worried just then – I heard it in your voice and could ascertain a worry.

JOHN. It's because I'm getting forgetful – I didn't want you to think that I was rude. Like if we had met before that perhaps you thought that I thought that you weren't interesting enough to remember. That I would make that sort of judgement on your character.

MARY 2. Is it a relief that we haven't met before?

JOHN. Well I don't want you to think that I'm a forgetter of people.

MARY 2. Why does that matter?

JOHN. It matters because it's not a very attractive trait in a person and it matters because we've only just met and first impressions are very important for human beings.

MARY *starts dropping in random sound cues – footsteps, country sounds, dogs barking, etc.*

MARY 2. What do you think people's first impressions of you are, John?

JOHN. That I'm a man...

MARY 2. Right.

JOHN. A tall ginger man – in relation to others I'm ginger and tall. And pale too – though everyone's pale in here.

MARY 2. And your character?

JOHN. Polite and even-tempered, most times. I don't like to use swear words – though some people find that threatening.

MARY 2. Why's that?

The DRUMMER *is making noises as he tunes his drums.*

JOHN. Well, Irish people love to swear – and when you don't do that often – they can be suspicious of you – you have to be careful.

MARY 2. It says here – you wanted to be a writer.

JOHN. I was never a writer.

MARY 2. But you wanted to be.

JOHN. There's no pens or pencils in here – apart from your pencil, of course.

MARY 2. Well, there couldn't be, could there.

JOHN. Sorry, what's your name?

Slight pause.

MARY 2. Mary.

JOHN. Ordinarily I'd love to not have people thinking about me, Mary – don't you think that's an easier way to live? That you exist – but you just exist enough so that you don't draw attention to yourself.

MARY 2. To be invisible?

JOHN. Right.

MARY 2. You'd be fine with invisibility, John?

JOHN. I dream of being invisible.

MARY 2. Do you dream about being invisible a lot then?

JOHN. Not often enough – but there have been dreams about invisibility.

MARY 2. Have you mentioned this to anyone else?

JOHN. I might have mentioned it to another actor once upon a time.

MARY 2. And how did they react?

JOHN. He couldn't really relate to it – what with visibility and audibility being essential to an actor's profession. He was pretty good at his job, I remember that.

MARY. Sure.

JOHN. Do you have a recurring dream, Mary?

MARY 2 (*she doesn't*). Yes... yes I do actually.

JOHN. Do you mind telling me what the dream's about? A personal story would help with matters of trust before we get started on my life.

MARY 2. Absolutely.

MARY 2 *looks at* MARY *and indicates that she should watch and learn how to talk to a person like* JOHN.

I dream, John...

MARY 2 *makes eye contact with the* DRUMMER *to accompany her story.*

...my recurring dream is that... (*Momentarily lost and must improvise.*) I am a lobster...

The DRUMMER *begins.*

...walking alone on a beach carrying a pail of milk... It's brimming over this milk and spilling down the sides of the pail. The beach, John, is empty but for me... and a few

minor crabs crawling about on the sand. In the distance…
I hear the sound of a huge horse galloping towards me.

MARY *makes clip-clopping noises with her hands into a microphone on her sound equipment.*

I place the pail of milk upon the sand – and looking up – and to my surprise – I see that the horse has no rider and yet has the face of a very handsome man. The horse is in fact… a centaur.

MARY *makes a centaur sound using the trolley mic – unsuccessfully.*

He begins to lick at my milk with his enormous lolling tongue.

MARY *makes a licking/slurping sound – successfully.*

Specks of milk fly and land and soak into the sandy-sand around the pail. Suddenly, John! – I'm ripping off my shell – lost in this feverish-fever-fever-frenzy… (*Starts getting out of her lobster costume.*) My God what's got into me! Jesus fucking Christ! The centaur looks up and shouts…

MARY (*into the trolley mic*). What the hell are you doing, Mary?

MARY 2. But I barely hear the centaur because I'm tearing off my protective exoskeleton and he needs to be significantly louder!

MARY (*as the centaur, louder*). WHAT THE HELL ARE YOU DOING, MARY!?

MARY 2. I definitely hear that – but I can't respond, John, because I'm lost in my own physical performance – something I learnt from three years in acting school! I'm out of my shell now and completely bollick-naked – (*She's not – she's in leggings and a* Wicked *musical T-shirt.*) and dancing on the sand like a caffeinated toddler at a children's party! The centaur returns to licking at my pail.

MARY*'s licking the mic.*

Faster he licks – faster I dance! Louder his licking!

MARY *licks louder.*

Milk is turning to cream and splashing out of the pail – pouring down the centaur's whiskery face. He starts to laugh.

MARY *starts laughing like a horse-centaur.*

Laughing loud!

MARY*'s almost yelling/laughing into the microphone.*

And louder even!

MARY *is red-faced – the microphone's suffering.*

Throwing back his enormous head and globules of – near-cheese – are flying from his chin and onto my ridiculously-expressive-sweating-dancing-naked-body. And then, John, and then… and then he faces me and he shouts…

MARY (*as the centaur, with sound effect*). COME MARY COME! RIDE ME! RIDE ME! RIDE ME!

MARY 2. I swing my leg over and onto his enormous back… And I ride that centaur as THE RED SUN BOILS THE UNSUSPECTING SEAAAAAAAAAAA!

The percussion stops – the DRUMMER *returning to tuning his drums.*

MARY *makes some clip-clopping sounds with her hands…*

Silence.

A long pause.

Then –

JOHN. Why were you dressed like a lobster just then?

MARY 2. It helped with the telling – it's all part of the performance magic.

JOHN. But even before you started talking about your dream – Why would you arrive here in a lobster costume?

MARY 2. I couldn't find my raincoat this morning when I left my house to catch the bus.

JOHN. But you found a lobster costume?

MARY 2. Never leave home without a coat, my agent always tells me – or a shell.

JOHN. So you're not on your way to somewhere else?

MARY 2. What do you mean by that?

JOHN. Not on your way to a children's party? It's just something I've heard before – actors not taking the testimonies seriously and hurrying off to play at children's parties…

MARY 2. We are here, John… John Kane… for you and for you only.

JOHN. Okay right.

MARY 2. We are each – us four – entrusted to one another – us and you. Does that make you feel happy?

JOHN. I think so yes.

MARY 2. 'Listened to'?

JOHN. Yes. Thank you, Mary.

MARY 2 *walks over to the sound trolley, rolls her eyes at* MARY *and whispers to her –*

MARY 2. Needy.

She lifts up the Lucozade bottle.

(*To* MARY.) The centaur. Excellent improvisational skills exhibited just then.

MARY. Thank you.

MARY 2. I meant from me.

MARY. Of course. Well done.

MARY 2. 'The red sun boils the unsuspecting sea.' Incredible words, powerfully delivered.

MARY 2 *drinks more Lucozade – like a calf suckling a teat.*

JOHN. I mentioned about the room not being particularly ready. That there's been a party of some sort –

JOHN *slightly appalled by* MARY 2*'s suckling.*

– I don't want to use up any of time cleaning it – but I don't want it to distract from what we're doing either – especially the banner which feels negligent...

MARY 2 *cradles and kisses the bottle of Lucozade like it was a baby –*

MARY 2. I love you too, my sweet. I love you – I love you – I love you – I love you – I love you – I love you – I love you – I love you – I love you – I love you – I love you...

JOHN *and* MARY *stare at* MARY 2.

Then –

Let's go!

MARY *claps her hands – a light only on* JOHN.

People are waiting – there's nothing to be scared about.

She sits behind the microphone.

JOHN. I'm always a little bit worried at the very start...

MARY 2. We've done this a hundred times – you're in excellent hands.

JOHN. Right.

MARY 2. Ready when you want to start.

A slight pause.

JOHN. Okay right.

During the below the three of them move around the space – the settings/staging loose – scenes fading in and out of darkness – the women a little inexpert in their theatre craft.

JOHN *slowly turns towards us – and with direct address – he begins his presentation.*

JOHN. My name is John Kane. I was born on the 7th of
February in St Michael's Hospital in Rathteelin.

MARY 2 (*to herself but unfortunately heard*). Oh God.

JOHN *hears this.*

He carries on.

JOHN. I'm the first and then the only child to a couple in their
early twenties. Rural town people and him a labourer of sorts
and her a wife and… a mother now.

MARY 2 (*prompting*). And music.

The DRUMMER *accompanies the below – building
atmosphere.*

JOHN. And out into the world and complications naturally and
slapped awake with no noise from me. And hours pass and
still this bluish colour – still silent I am – like a dead fish my
mother said when I was old enough to understand the joke.

MOTHER (*voice-over*). Have I ever told you how much you
looked like a dead fish in baby form?

TEENAGE JOHN (*voice-over*). Yes, Mother, you've told me
that one hundred times.

*A light comes up and we see the spoken action below – the
two* MARYS *playing the parts of his mother and father –
their backs to us – and wigs worn. They are slowly 'walking
away' – like practised mimes.*

JOHN. And in the hospital I stay behind in that tiny cot. And
had I seen my parents walk away from me through the ward?
Him searching his coat pockets for his beloved snuff –

MARY *loudly sniffs the back of her hand.*

– and her souring over those young nurses with their little
tiny hips.

MOTHER (*voice-over*). Little tiny bitches – little tiny hips.

*The phrase repeats and echoes, distorts badly, and fades
(thankfully) – as the light fades off the two* MARYS.

JOHN. Weeks they pass and spring comes early and through an open window and beyond the hospital – I can hear the outside world saying hello.

The sounds of countryside.

The sounds of birds and gentle breeze – of somewhere cattle chewing grass – all imagined from my tiny cot. And my blue skin fades as oxygen fills and colours me pink enough for him and her to return to me.

Quiet footsteps approaching – and we fade back up on the two MARYS *as mother and father –* MARY 2 *now wearing a 1940s ladies' felt hat.*

Their footsteps reheard through the ward. And finally lifted from the cot and placed into my mother's arms for that very first time.

The sound of baby noises.

Her skin? – it smells of rose and cigarettes – and we cut a line through the hospital us three. The ignored and quietly hated nurses – each one cooing my name – their tone proclaiming my doom.

NURSE 1 (*voice-over*). John.

NURSE 2 (*voice-over*). Oh, John.

NURSE 3 (*voice-over*). Poor John.

NURSE 4 (*voice-over*). Goodbye, John.

NURSE 5 (*voice-over*). John Kane. What a strong name.

The sound of the outside – a small country town.

JOHN. The glorious Irish outside – and a longing already to stay and play in its fields and climb in its trees while lit by its skies.

We see the action as MARY 2 *hands* MARY *a baby doll.*

By a bus stop and my mother hands me to my dad. And I stare up into his dead eyes – his upper lip – dusted in snuff-brown – those wet lips snarled like two slugs unhappily spooning one another at night-time. 'Her' an embittered queen of the small town – 'Him' an unlearnt rustic with infinite spite.

MARY 2 *and* MARY *expertly lip-sync their lines –*

MOTHER (*voice-over*). Come on then, Sean, let's get home to our miserable house.

JOHN. She says.

DAD (*voice-over*). Grand, love. You better take the little fella offa me – I think he shit himself again, Margaret.

JOHN. He says.

DAD (*voice-over*). Buckets and buckets of shite he has.

The light fades off the two MARYS *as* MARY *hands the baby doll back to* MARY 2.

JOHN. And 'home' we go. And none of her skin – none of her milk. I'm made fat over time from 'cow juice', Dad calls it.

DAD (*voice-over*) *and* JOHN. Give the boy some cow juice. He loves the cow juice, Margaret. Buckets and buckets of shite he has.

JOHN. And how quickly I've become accustomed to the silence. The song of my isolation played out in that box bedroom upstairs. The quietness fills that dour room. It lays heavy on every surface, every sheet. Within a week – it colours it all a terrifying black...

MARY 2 *enters* JOHN's *light with her script –*

MARY 2. Can we move it forward a bit, John?

The DRUMMER *stops playing.*

It's great, don't get me wrong – it's slightly underplayed but that's not really the issue. I looked ahead in the script and there's nothing of any great consequence for the next four or five pages.

JOHN. Okay.

MARY 2. It's nice and everything and the words especially are lovely – it's just not that important.

JOHN. Not important?

MARY 2. Your bath in the sink, maybe?

JOHN. But that's skipping some important details.

MARY 2. Yeah but at least it's dramatic – and it's good to get something of significance down.

JOHN (*not happy*). Right-fine…

MARY 2 (*prompting*). When you're almost one and nearing bath time…

JOHN. Yeah-yeah-okay.

MARY 2. Excellent though – great work.

JOHN. Thank you – you too.

A pause.

JOHN *turns back to us – settles himself – and continues –*

And it's winter time and in the kitchen and Mother's filling the sink with water for my bath –

We hear a tap running.

MARY 2 *leaves his light.*

MARY 2 (*prompting*). And music.

The DRUMMER *resumes.*

JOHN. And a cloud of heat is steaming the kitchen window and my knees are on the draining board, my small hands are sliding and marking the wet glass. Mother's snapping –

MOTHER (*voice-over*). Don't do that! Don't do that, John…!

JOHN. – and I turn it into a game until she's grabbing me and holding me down in the sink – in water a little too hot for the cold of the kitchen.

MOTHER (*voice-over*). Be still! Stop wriggling, John! Stop it!

JOHN. My legs are being scorched by the hot water and too shocked for tears. And how dark is the night outside these sweating windows. No memories back then beyond our garden – but there were neighbours and trees and fields and hills surrounding us – and on this night the deep silence of winter – the promise of snow in the hills. (*Slight pause.*) Her hand on my little back.

The sound of a baby/toddler by itself – is faded up.

She turns and leaves me alone in the kitchen sink.

I play with the same soap that cleans the pots and plates – and I turn its hard texture to pink mush in my little hands. The water losing heat over time – and again I look towards the kitchen door that she slammed behind her.

A door slamming sound – distant in his memory.

A light on MARY 2 *playing his mother sitting somewhere.*

I imagine my mother sitting in her own bedroom – her cigarette burning in her hand – her head in her other hand and lost in some dark disappointment.

The light fades off MARY 2.

I sat for over an hour in that sink. In that tepid grey and oily liquid I had cried but my voice had tired of crying. I knew that if I'd fallen from the sink to the floor there'd be more tears and red blood on the hard floor. (*Pause.*) To feel their arms around me… fall is what I did.

The faint sound of a baby/toddler crying hysterically is faded up.

DAD (*voice-over*). What happened to John, Margaret?

MOTHER (*voice-over, upset*). He's a stupid child – a stupid child!

A slight pause.

DAD (*voice-over*). Should we wash him in the sink again? – there's blood in his hair. Ah Jesus Christ…

The drumming stops.

MARY *claps her hands and the fluorescent lights come back on.*

A long pause.

The DRUMMER *walks away from his kit and leaves the room through the door.*

MARY *walks up to* JOHN.

MARY 2. An excellent beginning – well done, John.

JOHN. Thank you.

MARY 2. You would have been a wonderful writer had your circumstances been different – and you found yourself an editor. People will be happy, I think – (*To* MARY.) Don't you think that people will be happy and impressed even?

MARY. Well yeah they should be… it was well told, I thought… it was good.

MARY 2 *steps in closer to* MARY *– and gestures to* MARY *to step in closer to her.*

MARY 2. We've never worked with each other before, me and you, and we've only just met but I emm… (*Slight pause.*) I fucking hate the word 'Good'.

A slight pause.

MARY. Okay.

MARY 2 *steps back from her.*

MARY 2. Nice cueing of… (*Pronouncing each letter.*) S-O-U-N-D.

MARY 2 *pivots – and walks back to the booth.*

She opens the door – and the wind blasts out of the booth, propelling MARY 2 *backwards.*

She struggles to approach the door.

She enters the booth – closes the door – the light in the booth goes on – the wind has stopped.

JOHN *stares up at the 'Congratulations' banner.*

He gets a chair and places it beneath it.

He stands on the chair to take it down – but then looks at MARY.

JOHN. Why's your eyebrow like that?

MARY. Just something I'm trying that's all.

JOHN. Something actorly related?

MARY. Yeah.

JOHN. Like a character part?

MARY. Exactly.

A slight pause.

JOHN. What's your name?

MARY. Mary.

From the booth – MARY 2 *sees them talking. She doesn't like that.*

JOHN. Isn't she called Mary too?

MARY. Yeah.

JOHN. So you're two Marys?

MARY. That's right – we're two Marys.

MARY 2 *bangs on the booth window with a tennis racket.*

JOHN *rips down the 'Congratulations' banner.*

MARY *picks up her phone and presses it –*

Earth, Wind & Fire's 'September' comes on.

MARY *prepares some food for* JOHN *with bits of food on the party table.*

JOHN *brings his folded-up clothes into the cubicle and starts changing inside it.*

Meanwhile MARY 2 *is in the booth changing into a 1950s circle dress, putting on make-up, trying on a few wigs.*

MARY *knocks on the cubicle – and* JOHN *takes his medication from her – and then the small tray of 'food'.*

JOHN *closes the curtain in the cubicle and eats as he continues to dress – this becomes unnecessarily complicated.*

MARY *begins to dance to the music a little – just for her own entertainment.*

MARY 2 *leaves the booth (at 1.21 – the second verse) – fully and brilliantly costumed as* JOHN*'s mother.*

MARY 2 *watches* MARY *dancing to the music.*

MARY 2 *can't help herself – she begins to copy* MARY*'s steps.*

As the chorus kicks back in the two MARYS *dance in synchronisation.*

It's a competition.

Everything is.

MARY 2 *starts adding more difficult steps.*

After a while – MARY *stops dancing and just looks at* MARY 2 *continuing.*

At 2.24, 'September' begins to cross-fade – with composed music.

MARY 2 *stops dancing and picks up a microphone from the sound trolley.*

The fluorescent lights go out.

A spotlight comes up on MARY 2.

MARY 2 *starts to sing a song we don't hear.*

JOHN *sits down in the cubicle and puts on the headphones –
and begins talking to the interviewer.*

MARY *sits on the seat behind the small table and watches*
MARY 2 *'singing'.*

She gets up and looks in at JOHN *in the cubicle.*

JOHN *then notices that* MARY *is looking at him.*

MARY *turns away from* JOHN.

MARY *claps her hands and the fluorescent lights come on.*

MARY 2. You get the idea.

MARY. Right.

MARY 2. So what do you think?

MARY. Best not to sing it yourself, you don't have the voice for
it. Unless that's the point you're trying to make.

MARY 2 *walks up to* MARY *and caresses her cheek with
the back of her hand.*

MARY 2. Thank you for your honesty, darling.

MARY. Any time.

MARY 2 *grabs* MARY*'s eyebrow and rips it off her face.*

MOTHERFUCKER!!!

MARY 2 *hands her the eyebrow.*

MARY 2. You look a tiny bit younger than me.

MARY. I just look young, I'm not really. I never fixed you some
food – totally forgot.

MARY 2. Yeah well I don't eat solids.

MARY. Really?

MARY 2. Haven't eaten solids for ten years – it interferes with
my acting.

MARY. In what way?

MARY 2. In what way?!! Indigestion – bloating – wind. What age are you exactly?

MARY. Playing age – twenty-five to forty-five.

MARY 2. Are you with anyone romantically?

MARY. No of course not.

MARY 2. What do you mean by that?

MARY. Well, where would I get the time? People in our profession don't have other lives.

MARY 2. I've got another life.

MARY. What does it consist of?

MARY 2. This and that?

MARY. Nothing.

MARY 2. Everything.

MARY. Have you ever fallen in love?

MARY 2. I fall in love every day – everything we do is a love story.

MARY. Or a children's party.

MARY 2. Well, if you're good enough, yeah.

MARY. I want my own love story.

MARY 2. No you don't.

MARY. I do – I want to be in love.

MARY 2. Don't you enjoy doing what we do?

MARY. Yes, no – I'm tired.

MARY 2. Are we going to have a difficult time with each other?

MARY. I hope not, I don't have the energy.

MARY 2. It wouldn't be fair on John.

MARY. I agree.

MARY 2. John is our main concern – this isn't about me and you.

MARY. I know that too.

MARY 2. It's good that you know that – people are watching us.

MARY. D'you believe that?

MARY 2. What we're doing is of huge importance…

MARY 2's phone rings – the 'Willkommen' ringtone.

She answers it.

Hello. (*Slight pause.*) Yes. (*Slight pause.*) No no we're fine. She's fine. (*Slight pause.*) Thank you.

The call ends.

MARY 2 *looks back at* MARY, *who is staring over at* JOHN *again.*

What are you doing?

MARY. As a rule do you believe in the rumours?

MARY 2. No. Yes. What rumours?

MARY. I heard from a woman I know – another sound operator – and in between the work we had a discussion about free will and determinism.

MARY 2. And what were your conclusions?

MARY. We didn't have the intellect to reach any conclusions so we just ate cake, felt dreadful and waited until it passed.

MARY 2. And the rumours?

MARY. She had heard from this woman – that this other woman who was doing the work that we're doing – an actor like us…

MARY 2. Like me – you're a technician and a secondary actor. An extra, basically. Carry on.

MARY. That this actor didn't show up one day for work. She stayed on the bus and didn't get off. She vanished.

MARY 2. She probably died. People do die. Even actors. Why are you telling me this?

MARY. Because I'm feeling a little worried, I think.

MARY 2. Worried about what?

MARY. What we're doing maybe…

MARY 2. Have some Lucozade – that'll make you feel better.

MARY. I don't want any more sugar.

MARY 2. Of course you do – we love sugar.

MARY. Yesterday I had twenty-six teeth, this morning I counted twenty-five.

MARY 2. Well, that's one less thing to be worried about.

MARY. There are very few roles for toothless actors, Mary!

MARY 2. Yes but it's a requirement for theatre technicians – so that's perfect!

MARY 2 points to the sound equipment and snaps her fingers.

Go on then.

MARY walks back to the sound equipment.

MARY 2 sharpens the pencil in the pencil sharpener.

The DRUMMER *comes back through the door into the room with a Coke and Lion bar. He goes to his drum kit.*

JOHN *appears out of the cubicle and walks over to the bench stage-left.*

MARY drinks some Lucozade. Hates it. Must swallow it. Swallows it. Retches.

MARY 2 *stops with the sharpener.*

A beat of silence. Then –

Let's go!

MARY 2 *claps her hands – but the fluorescent lights remain on.*

She tries it again and the same result.

MARY *claps her hands and the fluorescent lights go out and only a light on* JOHN *sitting on the bench.*

Again – during the below JOHN *moves precisely around the space – the settings simple, faded in and out of darkness.*

In a marked contrast to the previous story – here everything is composed and beautiful – the two MARYS' *performances more nuanced.*

The sound of people entering a church.

We then hear the voices of Father McMahon and JOHN.

FATHER McMAHON (*voice-over*). Hello, John, how are you doin'?

JOHN (*voice-over*). Hello, Father.

FATHER McMAHON (*voice-over*). People around town have been saying that your mother's been preparing for the role of Mary Magdalene her whole life. We're awfully excited to see her performance in church this evening. Did she come with ya, John?

JOHN (*voice-over*). She had her make-up to put on – so she's walking behind with my dad, Father.

FATHER McMAHON (*voice-over*). She's fixing to sing us a song, I believe?

JOHN (*voice-over*). She is, Father, yeah – she'll be singing something.

FATHER McMAHON (*voice-over*). Mary Magdalene washing Jesus's feet with her own head-hair – sure there must be several appropriate songs for that, John?

JOHN. Yes, Father, there must be absolutely loads.

JOHN *stands up from the bench.*

MARY 2 (*prompting*). And music.

The DRUMMER *begins and plays the atmosphere beneath* JOHN's *story.*

JOHN *turns to us and continues.*

JOHN. I shuffle past Father McMahon and place myself at the back of the church – as my body occupies itself with neighbourly nods of recognition – and the insurmountable dread of my mother's imminent performance of Mary Magdalene on the altar.

FATHER McMAHON (*voice-over, from the pulpit*). G'morning, everyone.

CONGREGATION (*voice-over*) *and* JOHN. Morning, Father.

JOHN. I stay locked inside my head with big thoughts – where I return to – and churn again a memory that I'd woken up to for the past two thousand mornings. The memory is this.

MARY *presses a dry-ice machine on the sound trolley – it spits out its cloud.*

MARY 2. You are a thirteen-year-old boy, John.

JOHN. Right. And I was standing in my box bedroom in the soupy silence of my youth.

A light comes up on the two MARYS *as Mother and Dad –* MARY's 'Dad' *more costumed now.*

Another weekend ignored by him and her – and Monday mornin' and woken again in this half-wake, this sepia-toned world of mine – and I can hear my parents arguing through the partitioned wall –

DAD (*voice-over*). Why don't we do it any more, Margaret?

MOTHER (*voice-over*). You know why we don't!

DAD (*voice-over*). We shouldn't have had that boy! It's been a fucking disaster for years!

MOTHER (*voice-over*). I don't want you to touch me, Sean.

The light fades off them.

JOHN. And lying across my bedroom carpet like white moths –
my small lined notebooks packed with my words – are all
looking up at me. They start asking me difficult questions.
The house – groaning as usual, each surface talking and
deploring my fat life. My hands pull back the heavy curtain,
releasing the latch, the open window pushing in this heavy
mornin' breeze...

*The clear sound of a girl's breath – she seems to call
'John' –*

JOHN *listens to it – his eyes filling with tears.*

MARY 2. And not for the first time, be honest with us, John.

A light comes up on MARY *in the booth – her back to us,
her shoulders bare as she slowly dresses.*

JOHN. No not for the first time – I can see her standing at her
window inside her house across from our house. The curtain
is faint enough so I can see her outline, her morning shape
waking up like me, her name is Sarah – her age is thirteen
like my age. I watch her dress herself for school – and lean
into her back – her skirt being pulled and fastened around
her waist...

MARY 2. It carries you downstairs that image.

JOHN. It sits with me in our tiny kitchen, yeah.

*The morning radio is playing in the kitchen – faraway
mumbled voices.*

I fold open a notebook and I try to find words of 'love' in ink
that can't be spoken out loud. Sarah exists untouched by me
and the terrible darkness of our house. Like an angel she
floats above us.

DAD (*voice-over*). Doesn't he love his cow juice, Margaret?
Holy fuck – look at him go! Buckets and buckets of shite he
has. What are you writing in that little book, ya fool?

TEENAGE JOHN (*voice-over*). Just poetry.

DAD (*voice-over*). Poetry?! – ah Jesus Christ, Margaret! 'Tis poetry!

MOTHER (*voice-over*). Don't talk to John! I don't like you talking to him, Sean! I'm going to the city – this house is killing me.

The sound of a door slamming.

JOHN. My mother walks through our town trailing disgust. From her seat on the bus she carves out another her. She'll spend her day walking the city's concrete, lost in some fake romance – where men 'ooh' and 'ah' on cue. She'll return in the evening – and lie alone with herself on her bed. Her small noises and rose perfume will catch in the back of my throat – and have me running from my room and puking up on the grass outside. I'll turn my head up towards Sarah's window and I'll dream of her bare shoulders in her red dress.

A light comes up on MARY playing JOHN's teacher.

TEACHER (*voice-over*). Anois buachailli – open your books and read silently the next chapter for yourselves...

A light coming up on MARY 2 – 'Mother's' wig in her hand.

JOHN. There's a new boy on the other side of the class – and later on and in the yard Philip says to me –

MARY 2 *lip-syncs –*

PHILIP (*voice-over – he has a stammer*). Do you wanna co-co-come and play in my house, John?

JOHN almost overcome with emotion.

The sounds of children in the schoolyard are faded up.

JOHN. Other boys, the bigger and better boys – the boys who since my first days at school would jeer me over my 'sexy-lookin' mam' and mock me over my fatness and constant milky smell – those same boys – they twist their heads and scowl.

PHILIP (*voice-over*). My ma will pick us up in her ca-car, if you wanta, John.

JOHN. Where do you live, Philip?

PHILIP (*voice-over*). Way outta town there.

JOHN. And what beautiful words to hear and speak.

The sound of the car from the seats inside.

PHILIP (*voice-over*). Do you know what my favourite ca-car is, John?

TEENAGE JOHN (*voice-over*). No.

PHILIP (*voice-over*). Ferrari 250 G-GT.

TEENAGE JOHN (*voice-over*). Never heard of it.

PHILIP (*voice-over*). That's 'cause ya'd never find that sorta car in Ireland. Your dad doesn't have a car, does he, John?

TEENAGE JOHN (*voice-over*). Nah – he walks.

PHILIP (*voice-over*). You're good at school, aren't ya? At words.

TEENAGE JOHN (*voice-over*) *and* JOHN. Sometimes am – sometimes not.

The car sounds stop.

PHILIP (*voice-over*). Let's go and play in the woods over there. Do you know any girls in your town?

TEENAGE JOHN (*voice-over*). I know a girl called Sarah who lives right across the road from me.

PHILIP (*voice-over*). And what's she like, this Sarah?

JOHN. I come outside of myself and look at this different me walking side by side with Philip. The trees in the woods are loomin' ahead and offerin' us adventure in there. Language and new words and laughter – are batted back and forth between Philip and me, me and Philip. (*Slight pause.*) And then the air starts turning blue with made-up stories of Sarah. They mix these stories with strange images that I've seen of my mother in her bed. And Philip laughing at them – and questions asked and these stories start bending and twisting all rude around us – by me. Friendship is being knitted together with untrue scenes of Sarah. And thirteen years and my voice wakes into this new sound – that's free of the town, free of the old me. Free of silence this friendship.

A long pause.

Familiar school voices have travelled 'way outta town' too. They're walkin' through the woods t'wards us.

A BOY (*voice-over*). What are you doin' here outta town, John?

TEENAGE JOHN (*voice-over*). I'm here with Philip messin' around.

KEVIN (*voice-over*). Take your clothes off and we won't kill ya with this knife.

JOHN *begins to take his shirt off.*

TEENAGE JOHN (*voice-over*). I don't want to do that, Kevin.

PHILIP (*voice-over*). Do it, John – don't be a fucking idiot – take your clothes off.

TEENAGE JOHN (*voice-over*). You can kill me – I don't want to be naked out here.

KEVIN (*voice-over*). Sure, didn't we bring ya some other clothes to wear?

MARY *is holding out a red dress towards* JOHN.

A BOY (*voice-over*). We nicked it from that washin' line where that Sarah lives.

PHILIP (*voice-over*). Aw, your girlfriend! Ya don't mind wearing her clothes, do ya?

MARY *goes and hands the dress to* JOHN.

KEVIN (*voice-over*). Put on the dress and you can be our friend, John, we promise.

JOHN *puts the dress over his head – leaving his trousers on.*

A BOY (*voice-over*). Fuck he looks like his mam! Doesn't he look like his mother!!?

We hear laughter from the three boys.

KEVIN (*voice-over*). Now read us one of your love poems from your little book.

PHILIP (*voice-over*). Go on, d-do it, John!

JOHN. And I do read a poem of mine.

A pause.

Later – and when I'm made walk the four miles home in that dress – my head starts packing with words of blame against me for them rude stories that I made up about Sarah. Somehow my legs take me – the road conspiring with the world to lead me back to the town and all those people that hate me – lining up to see me.

A light comes up on MARY 2 *dressed as his mother. She holds a small syringe. She walks slowly towards him.*

The muffled sound of church is heard.

That day of me in that red dress looms big for six years. It wakes me every morning – and has me pukin' myself skinny. It fills my head again while we're all waiting for Mary Magdalene to make her big entrance. In that church at Easter week – all eyes are on my nineteen-year-old self as always. I can feel all those people. I can hear them using swear words about me and how I am. A thought comes to me like a bullet.

Below – the faraway sound of JOHN *screaming.*

It has me gathering every moment of silence in my life. Everything souring further and coloured black. It has me screaming out loud at the back of that church. I'm crying like a baby for those people. Like a loon. Like how the town and my parents have always seen me. I'm screaming into the blackness with this thought.

The drumming stops.

My head was never my own. Never once did it feel like mine.

MARY 2 *injects the syringe into* JOHN's *arm.*

MARY 2. Nice... -ish.

Brenda Lee's 'Emotions' starts.

MARY 2 *performs it – allowing Brenda the vocal – and lip-syncing the lyric.*

She improvises some choreography where she inhabits Mary Magdalene.

The DRUMMER *leaves his kit and leaves the room by the door.*

MARY 2 *pulls out a deflated red balloon from her cleavage. She begins to stretch it back and forth.*

She finds a pump from the trolley. The song continues. She pumps up the balloon.

The red balloon is heart-shaped. She hands it to MARY.

MARY 2 *slowly backs away towards the booth.*

MARY 2 *mimes a gun and points it over at the balloon.*

She 'fires her gun' and the balloon explodes in MARY*'s hands.*

As the song ends MARY 2 *throws open the door to the booth.*

A huge wind blasts and blows her over.

MARY 2 *battles to enter the booth.*

MARY 2 *enters the booth and as she closes the door – the light goes on.*

In the booth MARY 2 *starts getting out of her 'Mother' costume.*

The sounds of the institution can be heard outside the room.

MARY *stands looking over at* JOHN *– as he stares out at us.*

MARY. You okay?

A slight pause.

JOHN. D'you think they'll allow me leave?

He turns back to MARY.

MARY. I hope so.

A long pause.

Do you ever get to go outside?

A pause.

JOHN. I used to go to the walled garden – but I don't like to go there any more.

A pause.

MARY. What was the poem you read to them, John?

MARY 2 *hammers on the glass from the booth with the tennis racket.*

She makes a gesture to MARY *to 'shut up' – to play the next sound cue and get on with the work.*

MARY *walks to the sound equipment and hits a button.*

We hear JOHN *talking to the interviewer.*

INTERVIEWER (*voice-over*). How are you today, John?

A slight pause.

JOHN (*voice-over*). I'm fine, thank you.

A slight pause.

During the below – JOHN *gets out of the red dress and back into his shirt.*

INTERVIEWER (*voice-over*). How long have you been in here?

A pause.

JOHN (*voice-over*). I don't know.

A pause.

INTERVIEWER (*voice-over*). And what brought you here?

JOHN (*voice-over*). That's difficult to answer.

Composed music begins.

INTERVIEWER (*voice-over*). And whose idea was it that you'd come here, John?

A pause.

JOHN (*voice-over*). My parents and a doctor in my town.

A pause.

INTERVIEWER (*voice-over*). And what happened that ended up with you being here?

JOHN (*voice-over*). A man decided that this was the situation for me.

INTERVIEWER (*voice-over*). Did he tell you why?

A slight pause.

JOHN (*voice-over*). No he did not.

INTERVIEWER (*voice-over*). Has anybody told you why?

A slight pause.

JOHN (*voice-over*). No.

A slight pause.

INTERVIEWER (*voice-over*). Have you any idea why?

A slight pause.

JOHN (*voice-over*). Yes.

A slight pause.

INTERVIEWER (*voice-over*). And what is that?

A slight pause.

JOHN (*voice-over*). I'm not like other people.

The music has grown in volume and the taped conversation is lost.

MARY brings her script to the small table and reads ahead – studying it.

In the booth, MARY 2 is seen preparing a new character (a man) – changing clothes, wig, etc.

JOHN walks to the party table.

He fills a plastic cup full of water and drinks it.

MARY 2 then sees that MARY is reading the script.

JOHN suddenly turns over the party table.

He turns away and walks back over and into the cubicle – places on his headphones.

MARY 2 crashes out of the booth – slams the door shut.

The composed music cuts.

MARY 2 is costumed as the attendant, 'Liam' – she walks to the bottle of Lucozade.

MARY 2 drinks some Lucozade – places the bottle on the floor – and goes to do a number of press-ups over it.

She counts her press-ups.

MARY 2. One…

She strains badly – she may have a heart attack/stroke…

…Ten.

Managing one-and-a-half press-ups – she gets up and quickly goes to MARY and holds out the Lucozade.

Drink it.

MARY. I don't want to drink it.

MARY 2. Drink the fucking Lucozade and stop messin' around.

MARY. No, I don't want to.

MARY 2 opens the Lucozade, drinks it herself and spits it into MARY's face.

She places the bottle on the small table and walks back to
MARY.

With the headphones back on – JOHN *talks/listens to the*
interviewer.

MARY 2. Earlier when you said you felt worried about the
work that we were doing…

MARY. Right?

MARY 2. Why would you tell me that?

MARY. I thought it might be important.

MARY 2. And how do you feel now?

MARY. The same.

MARY 2. The same worries?

MARY. Maybe a little more worried.

MARY 2. And about what exactly?

MARY. I can't articulate them…

MARY 2. You're lying.

MARY. I'm not.

MARY 2. Why were you reading the script just then?

MARY. I was preparing for what's ahead of us.

MARY 2. For no other reason?

MARY. Like what?

MARY 2. Of all the people you worked with before – wouldn't
you say that I'm the most professional, the best actor…

MARY. Yeah, you're good.

MARY 2. 'Good' isn't a very good a criticism…

MARY. I know, I'm sorry…

MARY 2. 'Good' is a great distance away from 'Great'.

MARY. Right…

MARY 2. 'Good' is like punching an actor in the face. It's like shitting into that actor's mouth, removing their eyeballs and pissing into their brain – that's what 'Good' is!

MARY. What's your point?

MARY 2. I'm not making a point – I'm making colourful conversation.

MARY. Then what are we talking about beneath this conversation, Mary!?

MARY 2. Exactly.

MARY. I shouldn't have told you I was worried…

MARY 2. You made it my concern.

MARY. I know I did…

MARY 2. You're being unfair to John when you bring in an outside thought – do you understand me?

MARY. Yes!

MARY 2. So is that what you're doing, Mary?

MARY. I told you it wasn't a thought exactly but a feeling.

MARY 2. About what?

MARY. Our fucking purpose, Mary! I mean, look at us – in our show T-shirts and sporadic employment! When was the last time you actually felt something that might equate to a real-life experience…?

MARY 2 *slaps* MARY *hard across the face.*

That was completely unnecessar– !

MARY 2 *punches her in the stomach.* MARY *drops to her knees.*

JOHN *takes off the headphones and stands in the cubicle behind the curtain, listening to the exchange between the two* MARYS.

MARY 2. There are people watching us – aren't there people watching us right now, Mary?

MARY. Well, we don't really know that!

MARY 2. Producers keeping an eye on me and you – calling us on our phones.

MARY. Yes, definitely!

MARY 2. Are you clear of our purpose?

MARY. Yes!

MARY 2. The transaction between us and the people who've asked us to do this important work?

MARY. Is there not even a small part of you that can see that what we're doing in here is cruel to John!?

MARY 2 again slaps her across the face.

MARY 2. Deal with it!

MARY (*screams*). Fuck!

A slight pause.

MARY 2 watches MARY go into the booth – and begin to change into a new character.

The DRUMMER re-enters the room with another Coke and a Lion bar.

MARY 2 – claps her hands and the fluorescent lights go out ('Yes!') – a light only on the cubicle and JOHN.

The table light slowly/ominously comes up on MARY 2 sitting on the table as Liam.

She lip-syncs Liam's words.

LIAM (*voice-over*). What are you doing in the corridor, John?

A slight pause.

JOHN (*voice-over*). I thought I'd go for a walk. Go to the walled garden.

JOHN *steps out of the cubicle and the muffled sounds of the institution are heard – the cries, doors banging, etc.*

LIAM (*voice-over*). Have ya been a good boy lately?

JOHN (*voice-over*). I'm not a boy any more, Liam.

LIAM (*voice-over*). Why would you call me Liam? You're not allowed to call me by my name. Are you being cheeky to me?

JOHN. No.

LIAM (*voice-over*). You know what happens to cheeky people – what I have to do to them?

JOHN. Yes I know.

MARY 2 *leaves the table and walks over to* JOHN, *still lip-syncing Liam's words.*

LIAM (*voice-over*). Well, what happens to cheeky people? Tell me.

JOHN. They get hurt.

LIAM (*voice-over*). Have I ever had to hurt you, John?

JOHN. Yes many times.

LIAM (*voice-over*). And have you always deserved it?

JOHN. Yes always, Liam.

A pause.

MARY 2 (*prompting*). Music.

The DRUMMER *begins.*

JOHN. Where's the other Mary?

MARY 2. Do it – come on.

She kisses him on the cheek – and turns him so he's addressing us again.

JOHN. And against the hard ground – and against the walls and cracked ceiling – the words and noise of 'the left behind' – they crash. The long corridor takes me – its imperceptible tilt leading me past the unfortunate 'almost me's'. They're hunched over on their thin beds like unfinished statues – and fall into cries and screams and formless hurt all mixed by medicine. My brain like all of theirs – is slurred with past and present. I walk somehow.

MARY *comes out of the booth dressed as Valerie – her wig (blonde) subtly 1970s.*

JOHN. The smell of old blood and Liam – it congeals in the air and sits in the corridor. The door out to the walled garden. I step out into the outside-inside.

The sound of a gentle breeze – of a bird somewhere.

MARY *turns the bench so it's facing out.*

As she sits – a light comes up on her.

She looks out and mouths Valerie's words.

VALERIE (*voice-over*). I saw you from my room up there. I can see into the garden and you're here most days. I usually come down just after you leave, you know.

JOHN. Oh.

JOHN *sits with her.*

VALERIE (*voice-over*). Not that I didn't want to meet and talk to you – I did. I sort of teased myself with the anticipation of talking to you before actually talking to you.

JOHN. Oh.

VALERIE (*voice-over*). For two months I've been watching you come here and sit on this bench. I watch you stay for an hour and then I leave my room – and then I sit here and I try to think about what you might have been thinking about.

A pause.

VALERIE (*voice-over*) *and* MARY. How long have you been in here?

JOHN. To put a name on time seems cruel. It's one of the benefits of staying inside and living in a moderate climate.

We don't get the full expression of seasons – which would only mark a calendar's passing more clearly. I'm John.

VALERIE (*voice-over*) *and* MARY. I'm Valerie.

She takes his hand.

A long pause.

He sees her hand in his.

VALERIE (*voice-over*). What do you think about when you're sitting here on this bench, John?

JOHN. I don't want to think when I'm here. I know where the thinking will take me. When I was a boy, I always wanted to stop thinking but I never managed it.

A long pause – but the drumming continuing.

MARY *is looking down at his hand in hers. Tears fill her eyes.*

VALERIE (*voice-over*). Well, you can trust me – don't worry about any of that – I promise – I'm your friend.

JOHN *and* MARY *are both out of the scene.*

If you're worried – then don't tell Liam that me and you are good friends.

MARY 2 *leaves the bench and walks over to the booth.*

Despite her hesitancy – the door opens and closes without drama.

Inside the booth and MARY 2 *places a knuckle-duster on each hand.*

We'll talk about what we'll do – where we might go. The things we might see when we leave this place. My dad said I'll be staying only for a short time – that he has to get the house ready and then he'll come and collect me and I can come back home and we can forget that any of this has happened.

MARY *goes to the booth door and locks the door from the outside.*

Then I'll come back and get you – and then you can leave too. My dad will speak to the people keeping you here, John…

MARY turns off Valerie's voice-over – and the drumming stops.

A pause.

JOHN is standing and looking over at her.

JOHN. What are you doing, Mary?

Aaron Neville's 'Tell It Like It Is' begins to play.

MARY takes the microphone – and at the start she lip-syncs to Aaron's vocal.

MARY 2 sees/hears this and tries to open the booth door.

She can't.

She hammers on the booth's window and the light inside cuts out.

Suddenly a light only on MARY and JOHN – as she sings along with the vocal for him – an apology, maybe – but a longing for a love for herself, definitely.

MARY 2 crashes through the door, smashing its hinges – static interference blasts – obliterating the song.

The DRUMMER takes off – playing wildly.

MARY 2 goes to MARY and grabs her by the hair and drags her back into the booth.

She throws MARY to the floor.

We can't see MARY – but MARY 2 is hitting her with the tennis racket – over and over. The tennis racket smashes.

JOHN is terrified/panicking.

MARY 2 leaves the booth and pushes the sound equipment/trolley against the door – blocking MARY inside.

MARY gets back off the floor – her head bleeding.

The curtain blinds slowly roll down and cover the window into the booth.

MARY 2 *rips the last few pages from her script, grabs the table microphone and walks over to* JOHN.

The drumming suddenly stops.

MARY 2 *interrogates* JOHN.

MARY 2 (*reading*). 'And later and afterwards and I lie in my bed with thoughts of Valerie – with the faint smell of the garden still about me. Unnoticed – Liam is standing in the corridor. He'd seen me walk through the door from the outside-inside – where seconds before Valerie had walked all secret-smiled and glowing.' And then what?

JOHN. What do you mean?

MARY 2. What happened next?

JOHN. Directly next?

MARY 2. 'I eat with the others.'

JOHN *tries to turn to deliver the story to us.*

JOHN. And the noise against the hard ground…

MARY 2. To me!

JOHN. What?

MARY 2. You say it to me!

JOHN. And the noise against the hard ground, against the walls and the cracked ceiling… and facing one another…

MARY 2. 'And the food'…

JOHN. And what they call 'food' it arrives into our mouths unwanted. I pull back into my head – and avoid the corners where their medicine pushes me – in an untouched place I find again the sound of Valerie's voice.

MARY 2. And as promised!

JOHN. What do you mean?!

MARY 2. The next day, John.

JOHN. What's happened to Mary…?

MARY 2 (*shouts*). Music!

The drumming resumes – a different quality to the sound here – like JOHN *and* MARY 2 *exist in a bubble – a huge spatial sound world around them. A calmness.*

(*Reading.*) 'The next day and again down the corridor and again unnoticed is Liam standing there watching me – and again the door to the walled garden – to the outside-inside – I step…'

JOHN. And as promised she's sitting on the bench waiting there for me.

MARY 2. Hello, John.

JOHN. Hello, Valerie.

MARY 2. And you talk about what exactly?

JOHN. We talk about the outside and the getting out and the leaving. We talk about the size of freedom – of geographies yet seen…

MARY 2. 'My dad will be coming soon to get us.' And then?

JOHN. And then what?

MARY 2. 'And I return to my bed where Liam is sitting and waiting there for me' – and what is it that Liam said to you?

JOHN. That I should never speak to Valerie again…

MARY 2. 'I don't like to hit people – but I will if that's what it takes, John.'

JOHN. But I ignore his threats – and I walk the long corridor – its imperceptible tilt leading me past the half-alive – with blood dried in my mouth I open the door to the garden and to her.

MARY 2. And what secret dreams do you hold and only think and never say to her?

JOHN. Dreams where I return to my own town, to the people there, to my parents, to the deep silence of my youth.

MARY 2. And?

JOHN. To walk hand in hand with another – to walk through town with Valerie – to show and sour the mother who made me – to show and sour the man who called himself Dad.

MARY 2. And later and always.

JOHN. We meet in the walled garden, her and me. Other possible futures are spoken out between us – dull seasons pass unacknowledged...

MARY 2. It's love you're feeling.

JOHN. Until the day of the rain – it's love being built between me and her...

The sound of pouring rain fades into the soundscape. It's difficult for JOHN *to hear it.*

MARY 2 (*reading*). 'And the long corridor is walked – its imperceptible tilt is felt with the anticipation of Valerie.'

JOHN. I sit on the bench with God's rain thundering down and smashing out the remains of the old John's head. The last bit of hurt it washes from my brain and through my arms and legs and out into the ground it soaks – and fully alive I'm feeling.

MARY 2. And no her.

The rain surges.

JOHN. I look up to her window and there's a movement up there and then I see her and she's screaming. I can't hear what she's trying to say to me but behind the glass she's screaming and banging on the window – and I can see Liam somewhere in Valerie's room with her – she wants out, she's calling me to come and help her – he's grabbing at her...

Distant and we can hear audio of Liam attacking Valerie –

MARY 2. And did you go to her?

JOHN. I was too afraid.

MARY 2. Did you see her again?

JOHN. No never.

MARY 2. And what happened to Valerie, John?

JOHN. I don't know what happened to her.

MARY 2. Was it wrong that both of you met and spoke and
dreamt like this?

JOHN. Yes.

MARY 2. Do you deserve to be in here, John?

JOHN. Yes!

MARY 2. Do you need to be here, John?

Inside the booth the curtain slowly rises.

JOHN. Yes.

MARY 2. Is it right that people are keeping you in here and
helping you like this…?

JOHN. Yes, it's right.

It's raining in the booth and MARY *– blood streaming down
her face – is banging on the window to get out.*

*The sound and drumming and audio of Liam attacking
Valerie continues.*

MARY 2 *picks up her phone. Dials a number.*

MARY 2. Hello. It's me. (*Slight pause.*) Yes. (*Slight pause.*) Yes
it's finished.

The sounds stop.

The DRUMMER *gathers his things and leaves the room –
his work is done.*

JOHN *starts pacing – and then talking…*

JOHN. And winter time and in the kitchen and Mother's filling
the sink with water –

– a cloud of heat steaming the window – my small hands sliding and marking the wet glass – Don't do that! Don't do that, John! – and grabbing me and holding me down in the sink – Be still! Stop wriggling, John! Stop it! – legs are scorched by the hot water but no tears – I play with the same soap that cleans the pots and plates and turn its hard texture to pink mush in my little hands – I sat for over an hour in that tepid grey and oily liquid – and how dark is the night outside – no memories beyond our garden – but there were trees and fields and hills surrounding us – and on this night the silence of winter – the promise of snow – and made walk the four miles home in Sarah's dress –

The drums start playing by themselves.

– my head starts packing with words of blame against me for them rude stories I made up about Sarah – unseen unseen unseen – somehow my legs take me home, the bastards – the road conspiring with the world to lead me back to the town – in that church – all eyes are on my nineteen-year-old self – I can see them always – it has me gathering every moment of silence in my life – everything sours a colour black – it has me screaming out loud at the back of the church – (*Screams.*) I'm crying like a baby – like a loon – like how they always see me – I'm screaming in the blackness –

The Ghost of Sauris begins to creep back in.

– she leaves me in the sink – the water losing heat – the door she slammed behind her – my head was never my own – never once did it feel like mine – I pull back into my head but avoid the darker corners where their medicine pushes me – in an untouched place I find again the sound of Valerie's voice – of Valerie's face – always the outside and the getting out and leaving – we talk about the size of freedom – of geographies yet seen by us – Be still! Stop wriggling, John! Stop it! – I sat for over an hour in that tepid grey – legs are scorched by the hot water but no tears – Don't do that! Don't do that, John – unseen unseen unseen – how dark is the night outside – my head starts packing with words of blame against me – the water losing heat – the door she slammed behind her – the four miles home in Sarah's red dress – the road conspiring with the world to lead me – unseen unseen unseen – I'm screaming in the blackness – (*Screams.*) the promise of the snow in the hills – I avoid the corners where their medicine pushes me – Stop wriggling, John! Stop wriggling! – the glorious Irish outside – and a longing already to stay and play in its fields and climb in its trees while lit by its skies – unseen – the glorious Irish outside – and a longing already to stay and play in its fields and climb in its trees while lit by its skies – the glorious Irish outside...

MARY 2 *hits a switch on the sound equipment and the above words, spoken by* JOHN, *arrive out cut up and mangled. From some sort of sense – the words quickly lose all definition...*

Kjfheighipeghipruhgipughierughihgihieripughierubverbigker jbfeurfiebierubeirbeirgbiergbegbfehfguerucbuhfbhbhebvehb bhflejhfblhrblehrjbgjlehbrljehbrfhbfhebrfjhrebfjhfbjhbrhfjhrf jhrbfjbvfjhfjqhebfhqerferfvehrfvehvhjlqvqhrefvhvehrfvhjvqh fhrvfhjqvqhrvfhqvqhfvqhfvqhvfqhfvqhvhqfvhqfvuhqvquhrf vquhrfvquhrefvuqhrvfuhqvfuiqhvfquihvfquihvqiuhvquirhfvq uhfviqufvquhuqviuququhvquhrfvuqrqufrfvwouyqvyfrvqfhwf qwhrfvqfhvoufouwqfowqufovfouvffv

MARY 2 *is filming* JOHN *on her phone.*

Through the above – JOHN *continues to call out – 'the glorious Irish outside – and a longing already to stay and play in its fields and climb in its trees while lit by its skies' – but these words are being eaten and lost by the recorded and edited* JOHN.

The light in the booth comes back on.

MARY *is banging on the window to get out.*

The chopped-up audio continuing – relentless.

MARY 2 *looks on impassively.*

MARY 2 *pushes back the sound trolley and* MARY *comes out of the booth and goes directly to* JOHN *– but he is out of control and she must stay back from him.*

MARY 2 *stops the audio.*

Silence.

JOHN *collapses on the ground.*

A long pause.

MARY 2 *switches on another piece of audio – and during the below she puts back on her lobster costume.*

We hear a recording.

INTERVIEWER (*voice-over*). How are you today, John?

A long pause.

We then hear JOHN *as a much older man in his eighties.*

OLDER JOHN (*voice-over*). I'm fine, thank you.

A slight pause.

INTERVIEWER (*voice-over*). How long have you been in here?

A pause.

OLDER JOHN (*voice-over*). I don't know.

A pause.

INTERVIEWER (*voice-over*). And what brought you here?

OLDER JOHN (*voice-over*). That's difficult to answer.

A pause.

INTERVIEWER (*voice-over*). And whose idea was it that you'd come here, John?

A pause.

OLDER JOHN (*voice-over*). My parents and a doctor in my town.

INTERVIEWER (*voice-over*). And what happened that ended up with you being here?

A slight pause.

OLDER JOHN (*voice-over*). A man decided that this was the situation for me.

INTERVIEWER (*voice-over*). Did he tell you why?

A slight pause.

OLDER JOHN (*voice-over*). No he did not.

Fully dressed as the LOBSTER – MARY 2 *turns off the audio.*

She looks at JOHN *and* MARY.

MARY 2. Right. Good.

She leaves the room – the door remaining open.

MARY *looks at* JOHN.

About the audio –

JOHN. Is that me?

A slight pause.

MARY. Yes, John.

A slight pause.

JOHN. Play the rest of it.

MARY goes to the sound equipment but before she can get there – it switches itself on.

INTERVIEWER (*voice-over*). Has anybody told you why?

A slight pause.

OLDER JOHN (*voice-over*). No.

A slight pause.

INTERVIEWER (*voice-over*). Have you any idea why?

A slight pause.

OLDER JOHN (*voice-over*). Yes.

INTERVIEWER (*voice-over*). And what is that?

OLDER JOHN (*voice-over*). I'm not like other people.

INTERVIEWER (*voice-over*). What do you mean by that?

A slight pause.

OLDER JOHN (*voice-over*). People dislike me because I'm not completely like them.

INTERVIEWER (*voice-over*). And why are you not like them, John? Who tells you that?

A pause.

OLDER JOHN (*voice-over*). Other people tell me.

The taped interview stops by itself.

A long pause.

JOHN whispers to himself.

JOHN. How long have I been here?

He looks at MARY.

A pause.

There's never been anyone listening. It's just us. People like you.

A pause.

JOHN closes his eyes.

Then –

And heavy rounded in that hurt
In darkness there a million times.

Behind the cloud the sun it came
And saw his shape –

And how it shined.
And in the sun the past it fades
And gone the silence sorrow made
The boy will live and days will ease
And love will walk –
Upon the breeze.

JOHN *looks back at* MARY.

A long pause.

MARY. You want me to stay as long as I can, John?

A pause.

JOHN. Yes please, Mary.

MARY *sits beside him.*

After a thirty seconds – JOHN *takes her hand in his.*

They sit in silence – and we watch them for a whole minute.

The music finishes.

The room and they – are still.

Blackout.

The End.

THE SAME

The Same was first produced by Corcadorca Theatre Company at the Old Cork Prison, Cork, on 13 February 2017, and subsequently as part of Galway International Arts Festival at Galway Airport on 18 July 2019. The cast and creative team were as follows:

LISA	Catherine Walsh
THE OTHER LISA	Eileen Walsh
Director	Pat Kiernan
Designer	Owen Boss
Composer & Sound Designer	Peter Power
Lighting Designer	Mick Hurley
Photography	Enrique Carnicero
Producers	Fin Flynn
	and Rachel Gleeson

Funded by the Arts Council of Ireland

Characters

LISA
THE OTHER LISA

Lights up.

A metronome is heard beating at 100bpm.

On a stage – two grey tables – side by side – a five-foot gap between the tables.

A plastic water jug on each table and a plastic cup.

From either side of the stage two women enter and sit down.

Sitting behind the stage-right table is LISA.

Sitting behind the stage-left table is THE OTHER LISA. *She's younger than* LISA *by a number of years.*

The metronome stops.

THE OTHER LISA. I'd been to the city before with the Girl Guides and it rained. It mightn't have rained. It probably did rain – it always rains. Four out of five days it rains. The one thing I remember correctly was that I bought a chocolate bar with marzipan in the middle – or maybe a bar of marzipan with chocolate on the outside. That was the day I learnt that I hated marzipan. I can remember that and not very much else. But that was a different day and not a very significant day. Not the day that we're interested in. So as I stepped off the train into the new city I thought about the marzipan day – and that awful taste of marzipan having slept somewhere in the back of my throat, lying dormant like a giant almond bear – it woke and threw up – not just the memory of my trip with the Girl Guides back then – but it threw up a little of that egg sandwich I had hastily consumed in the dining carriage. So that day – the day of my arrival – the day we're interested in – my first feeling was of dread for this city. It may have lasted a few seconds and no more than that. Certainly that egg-puke-taste subsided and was replaced by something graver – but the dread was real – was felt real.

Right at the back of my throat and it slid further and grabbed my heart – and further still it slid and sat in my stomach like a bomb.

An aggressive change of light.

The sound of a voice being forwarded very fast.

It lasts three seconds and stops.

LISA. It was a normal day in that it was raining outside. Four out of five days it rains. Not that I had seen the rain – 'cause it wasn't raining just yet. I could smell it. The probability of rain and what it was to dress accordingly in this city with ninety per cent precipitation had me looking at my clothes. In response to a late-night call from Gavin I wore a heavier sock. If not a day's work – at least a morning's work on the sandwiches was promised. A key to a happy life is a happy foot – I read those words a long time ago. They were stitched into a cuddly toy I had that was in the shape of a foot. Unsurprisingly I never took to cuddling that foot – but daily I live by its philosophy. An unimportant, uneventful morning of washing and eating and staring out my window in anticipation of the probability of rain. And then it did. In buckets it did.

An aggressive change of light.

The sound of a voice being forwarded very fast.

It lasts ten seconds and stops.

You're going to feel nervous and that's fine.

THE OTHER LISA. That's normal, I said.

LISA. Because it's a new city you're going to.

THE OTHER LISA. A fresh start, you mean.

LISA. You wouldn't be normal if you didn't have worries.

THE OTHER LISA. I'd worry if I didn't have them.

LISA. Before is in the past.

THE OTHER LISA. And I shouldn't live in the past.

LISA. Well, you can't – we've talked about this before.

THE OTHER LISA. Yes we did, Claire, I said.

LISA. We can acknowledge that things have happened – but that was then. That's what we've talked about, Lisa.

THE OTHER LISA. I know that.

LISA. You can't forget completely of course.

THE OTHER LISA. It will always be there somewhere.

LISA. You have to learn to cope. It's perfectly normal to feel worried.

THE OTHER LISA. I am worried – and I want to be normal.

LISA. This new city you're starting out in is brand new.

THE OTHER LISA. It's a new journey we decided.

LISA. Completely new, she said.

THE OTHER LISA. Well, not exactly new, Claire. When I was ten and in the Girl Guides I bought some marzipan there.

LISA. Oh right…

THE OTHER LISA. I hate marzipan.

LISA. I know.

THE OTHER LISA. It feels very unnatural to me. About a million miles away from an almond. No amount of chocolate can disguise marzipan for what it is, Claire.

LISA. It's a new Lisa we're talking about, Lisa.

THE OTHER LISA. Yes.

LISA. Do you understand me?

THE OTHER LISA. Yes of course – I'm not fucking stupid!

LISA. Good girl, she said.

THE OTHER LISA. There were sights and the map came to life
– and I might have marvelled about that. And there was a
different accent, certainly – and those who looked – I felt
fear – and those who didn't look – I felt something,
definitely. In hindsight – I probably needed to eat. If I
walked around with an empty stomach I was a vessel for all
sorts of dread. Mother told me that. She said I didn't need a
therapist – I just needed a selection box. There was some
truth in that – but then selection boxes are just for Christmas
and what the fuck am I supposed to do from mid-January
onwards?!

LISA. You're Lisa.

THE OTHER LISA. I was told this by Howard.

LISA. Was it a nice journey, he asked.

THE OTHER LISA. Aspects of the journey were nice. I can't
remember what they were. It was a mixture of sensations.
Most of it was not too horrible, Howard.

LISA. Well, that's good.

THE OTHER LISA. Yes it is good.

LISA. Have you been to this city before, Lisa?

THE OTHER LISA. It seemed pointless going into the story of
the Girl Guides and marzipan so I said No – which in this
new world where I'm dismissing my past – was actually a
truth.

LISA. There's a booklet on your desk – it's called Guidelines –
which are strict rules – but we're not strict – it's not that sort
of place, he said. As residents we talk about respecting one
another – that sort of thing's really important, really.

THE OTHER LISA. A small blue room.

LISA. Respect not only washes dishes and mops up water that
might have splashed onto the floor risking accidents –
respect allows the residents to have different opinions, you
know what I mean, don't you, Lisa?

THE OTHER LISA. Yeah of course. Respect's really important.

LISA. It is really important.

THE OTHER LISA. I know it is – you just told me that it's really important, Howard.

LISA. That's because it really is.

THE OTHER LISA. Do I have a key to my bedroom to lock myself in?

LISA. Let me introduce you to Everyone. Everyone – this is Lisa.

An aggressive change of light.

The sound of a voice being forwarded very fast.

It lasts three seconds and stops.

There were nearly other occasions when he nearly asked – but when he asked – well, I was surprised – not by the asking but the circumstance which led to the asking. I want to say glandular fever but I'm not altogether sure if it was that or what that was – or what that is – even now glandular fever's a complete mystery to me.

THE OTHER LISA. So?

LISA. Will she be back? I asked

THE OTHER LISA. Not today.

LISA. I mean in the future, Gavin – will she be back in the future?

THE OTHER LISA. Let's just worry about this morning.

LISA. She's done aqua-aerobics.

THE OTHER LISA. Okay.

LISA. Which might account for her glandular fever.

THE OTHER LISA. It may not be glandular.

LISA. It might be something else then.

THE OTHER LISA. Glands are complicated, Lisa.

LISA. I'm not altogether certain what glands do.

THE OTHER LISA. They release stuff, he said.

LISA. My God, really?

THE OTHER LISA. They're regulators basically.

LISA. Poor Avril – what a terrible surprise.

THE OTHER LISA. The question I'm asking you is – Can I rely on you this morning, Lisa?

LISA. There's been very few certainties in my life – so the word 'yes' arrived emblazoned. There can be nothing more strengthening than that word – and to say it in that circumstance – to crown that question with such complete certainty. I found myself following yes with another yes – and then possibly over-egging my response with a – Yes, Gavin – and even further again – Yes, Gavin, I will be responsible for the tea and sandwiches at today's funeral!

THE OTHER LISA. Good girl.

LISA. A ham sandwich can soothe a heart – a cup of tea can recalibrate a life – a sausage roll can sedate a tragedy. Funerals are wonderful occasions for caterers. Of course I would have remembered this funeral even before I met The Other Lisa – it would have always been significant because of my nomination – even before The Other Lisa's late arrival into that dead woman's kitchen.

An aggressive change of light.

The sound of a voice being forwarded very fast.

It lasts three seconds and stops.

THE OTHER LISA. The probability of rain and what it was to dress accordingly in this city with ninety per cent precipitation had me looking at my clothes hung up. Not that there was a plan to leave the blue room – hadn't reached that thought – sometimes the body takes over and has me dressed

before I've had a chance to think. Upright and deodorised
and I'm sitting around the table with my housemates and
stuck in a conversation about Coco Pops with a shouty
woman. She never did learn to eat with her mouth closed and
cereal is poppin' from her gob like dark shrapnel. I can hear
Howard at the worktop dishing out the medication into little
eggcups – Thank Christ – I can hear the rain beginning to
spit at the window in expectation of buckets.

An aggressive change of light.

The sound of a voice being forwarded very fast.

It lasts three seconds and stops.

Ordinarily we'd have it in the living room – but it seems
undignified to lay out sausage rolls where moments earlier a
dead woman was laid. Her daughter, maybe – just behind me
and leaning at the kitchen door frame like a plank. Is it only
you and Gavin, Gavin and you? And just you on the
sandwiches – no other girl with ya? I nodded but then quickly
shook my head. We've been promised enough sandwiches, by
the way. Her niece, I think. Definitely her niece. We've been
promised sausage rolls. The bereaved are awfully unstable
and unknowingly desperate for sustenance – for that reason I
don't respond and stay busy with the cheese spread. Just
make sure the pastry's crispy that's all. She goes and I sense
another behind then – standing there like a lone penguin – her
feet splayed at ten to two. Our first conversation is –

I'm sorry I'm late.

LISA. You're late.

THE OTHER LISA. I know I am I'm sorry. It was the bus. It
    was the rain. A combination of both.

LISA. All right.

THE OTHER LISA. There's a lot of people in there. In there in
    the living room.

LISA. I know that.

THE OTHER LISA. Gavin said it's a funeral.

LISA. It is a funeral.

THE OTHER LISA. Where's the coffin then?

LISA. In the ground. This is called the afters.

THE OTHER LISA. Why do they call it that?

LISA. Because it's after the funeral.

THE OTHER LISA. Oh yeah. Is it sad in there in that room?

LISA. People die all the time.

THE OTHER LISA. What does that mean?

LISA. It's only sad for a moment. It passes. In the scheme of things, it's hardly sad at all.

THE OTHER LISA. My mother's just died. I'm on my own now, sort of.

LISA. You think you can wrap those cocktail sausages in pastry and stick them in the oven till golden?

THE OTHER LISA. You mean – can I manage it?

LISA. Right.

THE OTHER LISA. Right.

LISA. I'm Lisa.

THE OTHER LISA. Really?

LISA. Yeah.

THE OTHER LISA. I'm Lisa too, I said.

LISA. And nothing to suggest what would happen next and after. And maybe I felt something like she felt it – but maybe wrapped in pastry and rolled in grief – or spread beneath that spreadable cheese that something. Was it already growing in the kitchen – was it beating down a track to that bench by the lake and towards all that FUCKING MADNESS!?

An aggressive change of light. The sound of a voice being forwarded very fast.

It lasts three seconds and stops.

THE OTHER LISA. There would be people naturally – which brings its own complications, said Howard – but I needed out – I needed to get out and do something. So when he asked I said yes before I had a chance to say nothing. I said yes and found myself on a bus with a freshly ironed skirt and blouse. I made the excuse – It was the rain. It was the bus. A combination of both.

LISA. Right.

THE OTHER LISA. But that was a lie. People were queueing up in the garden to get into the house and out of the wet – and shrunken from the grief they were – and soaked from the cemetery.

LISA. Lisa, he called!

THE OTHER LISA. I held back – looking like a lone penguin out on the street – that grief like some force field – pinning me back – wanting me to turn on my flat feet and head back to the home. And if I did – if I turned and walked – if we never met – would things have spun out the same!?

LISA. Lisa.

THE OTHER LISA. And Gavin's arms waving at me to come.

LISA. Into that kitchen and get preparin' the food like a good girl.

THE OTHER LISA. And turning away from the table with her spreadable cheese – our first conversation then.

LISA. You're late.

THE OTHER LISA. It was the bus. It was the rain. A combination of both.

LISA. There's a lot of people in there. In there in the living room.

THE OTHER LISA. Gavin said it's a funeral.

LISA. It is a funeral.

THE OTHER LISA. Where's the coffin?

LISA. In the ground. This is called the afters.

THE OTHER LISA. My mother's just died. I'm on my own now, sort of.

LISA. Well it's only sad for a moment, they say.

THE OTHER LISA. Oh I'm not sad – not sad a bit.

LISA. You think you can wrap those cocktail sausages in pastry – and stick them in the oven till golden?

THE OTHER LISA. Unheard that last line.

LISA. I'm Lisa, by the way.

THE OTHER LISA. Really, I said?

LISA. Yeah.

THE OTHER LISA. Only part-hearing that line about the cocktail-sausage-golden-oven set in motion a series of events that saw bereavers standing in the living room and sucking on uncooked pastry and biting into frozen sausages. And Gavin's arms jabbing then – and a series of words thrown about the kitchen but spat in my direction.

LISA. Uncooked. Dope. Stupid. Fool. Christ. Pastry. Thicko. Moron. Loon. Twit. Get. The. Fuck. Out. Of. This. Fucking. Kitchen.

THE OTHER LISA. Which ordinarily would upset – would see me racin' to my residential – would see me bury my head in my pillow and praying for death!

LISA. You're fired, he said.

THE OTHER LISA. None of it was heard – not a word – well barely heard – beneath a universe of something else – at that stage – unexplainable this something else – but a need to be with Lisa – to breathe the same air as Lisa – to walk the same step – to get the same bus.

An aggressive change of light.

The sound of a voice being forwarded very fast.

It lasts three seconds and stops.

LISA. Do you have another job to go to?

THE OTHER LISA. No.

LISA. So what will you do for money, I asked.

THE OTHER LISA. I don't need money – I have help – there are people who help me. Helpers. I just need to get out once and a while – which I can – which I am now.

LISA. Right.

THE OTHER LISA. Do you like this city?

LISA. A valuation of something is difficult for me. Aspects of the city I like. I can't remember what bits. It's a mixture of many sensations. Why are you looking at me like that?

THE OTHER LISA. Like what?

LISA. Like longer than is necessary.

THE OTHER LISA. Don't you think we look the same?

LISA. No.

THE OTHER LISA. Not the exact same – just the...

LISA. What?

THE OTHER LISA. There's similarities, I said.

LISA. No there isn't.

THE OTHER LISA. In the eyes – and the head too – and maybe the chin and the nose.

LISA. She's talking fast.

THE OTHER LISA. Facially we're very similar, me and you. But not the exact same – but similar only, don't you see that at all?

LISA. No not at all.

THE OTHER LISA. Or maybe just…

LISA. What, I said.

THE OTHER LISA. Something else – something invisible –
don't you see that?

LISA. Don't I see something invisible?

THE OTHER LISA. See meaning sense, I mean. Don't you
sense a similarity between us?

LISA. She said.

THE OTHER LISA. I felt it immediately when I was in that
dead woman's kitchen – didn't you feel it too – it started just
then when I said my mother just died?

LISA. Maybe you need to eat something, I said, wanting it to stop.

THE OTHER LISA. Why do you say that?

LISA. If you walk around with an empty stomach you're a
vessel for all sorts of dread.

THE OTHER LISA. My mother said that.

LISA. Oh.

THE OTHER LISA. I ate one of those uncooked sausage rolls I
failed to cook – there's nothing in me but dough and pig bits.

LISA. This is my stop.

An aggressive change of light.

The sound of a voice being forwarded very fast.

It lasts three seconds and stops.

THE OTHER LISA. And later and a few days later and
incredibly no rain – and not much going on and more
residential than outside walking-about – apart from a day trip
to Tesco – the ground dry and dusty then – the trip
unimportant. And late mornings in bed and medication with
meals – and avoiding the shouty woman with her talk of

Coco Pops – but later and dinner at seven with the gang they call us – come on the gang – the gang's all here – like we have the choice to form ourselves into a gang. And chickpeas à la Howard – and the dinner conversation unheard like radio in another room – what with my mind still on Lisa, you see – or rather Lisa in my mind. I'm finished first and I'm in the living room by myself – and television murmuring, its picture unseen – and just me standing still and looking at the big collage of photos on the wall beneath the words PEOPLE WE LOVE – and memories and years cut up and stuck down faces of other residents past – the proverbial wall of shame – and stepping in to see for the first time – a face in that collage – and it's my face – my exact face – the same face as mine – and spelled out with gold ink underneath – Lisa.

An aggressive change of light.

The sound of a voice being forwarded very fast.

It lasts three seconds and stops.

LISA. And later and a few days later and incredibly no rain – and not much going on – and late mornings in bed and medication is taken with meals – and my trips, I call them little trips – and walking the city in the usual manner – the exact manner. And nothing from Gavin with his business relegated most likely – his name is hanging over the city and spelled out in uncooked pastry. G-A-V-I-N. And daily there's a constant inside here – and not wanting to put a name on the constant for fear of it unravelling – and still no rain – and dry and dusty the streets – and through the window – my window on the third floor – and she's standing at the bus stop outside but not taking the bus or any bus – which tells me that the constant has been there since that dead woman's kitchen – like it arrived invisible in the air with The Other Lisa. The events of the uncooked sausage rolls I remember as mine, you see – but as mine in my past way back – as once done by me! Christ! She's standing there in the car lights. She's looking up at my looking back.

She stops.

To talk. (*Pause.*) We must talk.

A very long pause.

LISA *smashes her open palm on the table – to hurt herself.*

An aggressive change of light. The sound of a voice being forwarded very fast.

It lasts twenty seconds and stops.

The sound of the interior of a fast-food restaurant and muzak playing.

THE OTHER LISA. I'm wearing a Disney frock because that's what she calls it – but it's not Disney and really it's not even a frock – it's something she pulled together an hour before I was made to wear it. (*Pause.*) Do you remember that birthday, Lisa?

A slight pause.

LISA. Yeah, of course.

Music.

THE OTHER LISA. Go on.

A pause.

LISA. In that frock I'm standing in the bedroom and I hear her open the door to children's voices – and a little stalled and confused they are – children she asked just the day before to my party – children I don't know.

THE OTHER LISA. And the faces of those children's mothers who leave them with her and those other mothers who stand in our flat and twitch.

A pause.

LISA. And then her turning up the radio loud – and awkward games of Musical Chairs and Pass the Parcel – and some children pulled from our flat by nervous parents –

THE OTHER LISA. And other children – not yet too frightened – grinning at her but their eyes are on their mothers.

LISA. I ask her can I get out my Disney frock – that the collar's way too itchy – but unheard by her as she heats the food.

THE OTHER LISA. And a little girl…

LISA. Amy, I think.

THE OTHER LISA. Right. She takes me to our toilet and says that we can change clothes.

A pause.

And then what?

A slight pause.

LISA. And Amy wears the Disney frock and I wear her red jumper and jeans and we step out of the toilet – the room empty – the borrowed children are all gone – escaped, Amy whispered. And she's sitting at the table – picking at it with her fingers – looking at the birthday cake bound in hard plastic. She's hitting me hard then and pulling the Disney frock back over Amy's head. And there's screaming of course and jumbled sharp words – and Amy's mother and the door opening – and lifting out her child – and how I wanted to be held like that.

A slight pause.

And later and it's her turn to cry, of course – and her wanting to be with me, she said it in that voice. I want to be with my little girl.

A pause.

It felt good when she died.

A pause.

THE OTHER LISA. I saw a picture of you in the home. We're you in the same blue room too, the same bed as I'm in now?

A slight pause.

LISA. Yeah.

A slight pause.

THE OTHER LISA. How do we have the same memory, me and you?

A slight pause.

Can we be the same person, Lisa?

The music and fast-food noises rise in volume.

They suddenly cut.

An aggressive change of light. The sound of a voice being forwarded very fast.

It lasts twenty seconds and stops.

THE OTHER LISA *remains silent –* LISA*'s delivery is even and measured.*

LISA. We start meeting by the lake on the edge of the city – on this bench we sit and talk and begin to knit together what was. With each word the city starts fading into her and me. Together we fall into our past life and into these moments where we were alone – into each other's skin and heartbeat. Into those places where we were before. And to speak and to be understood by another. To hear another one speak of what I felt and thought and barely understood till now. To be in this past and feel now understood wholly. Past life gathers around us. Words start knitting into one another and slowly begin to pull the past ever closer. We arrive and sit with sandwiches – our breaths saved to talk to one another. And early to sleep – and calls from Gavin unanswered. And still no rain since the day we first met – and every waking moment wanting to be sitting on that bench with The Other Lisa – and hearing my voice and thoughts returning to me. And there are weeks of this in the sun – until one day we're sitting on the bench as always and I'm listening to a detail of my life when I was a child and living in that flat with the woman I hated calling Mother. And hearing yet another story – I look away as Lisa talks – and the city is disappearing fast around us.

THE OTHER LISA. She's quiet then.

LISA. It's disappearing, I say to her. Around us our past has started to blot out all that was once new to me – all this new life I've been making for years in this city.

THE OTHER LISA. She's quiet, I think.

LISA. The day I stepped off the train for the first time with feelings of dread and thoughts of that marzipan – that day – a day filled with dread but a day that was still made new by me – a new start.

THE OTHER LISA. Lisa, what is it?

LISA. That day too is being covered with stories of the old city and how I was and how things always were. From the bench we talk and cover my new life made here in this city and pulled back into everything I once was – everything I ran from.

THE OTHER LISA. Lisa?

LISA. She speaks in words that I would speak, in a voice that I would use, about a life that I once lived – and all that I made new in this new city is being covered with something I tried to forget – and covered by me, by her talk, by us.

A long pause.

No.

An aggressive change of light. The sound of a voice being forwarded very fast.

It lasts twenty seconds and stops.

THE OTHER LISA. And sitting on the bench – and not yet then… whatever – not yet?… difficult to put a word on it. And distracting myself with the lake – with the ducks – with a city unseen by me, really – but waking, I imagine – and waking into another rainless day, by the sense of it – another dry day and the city waking into this dust. And resting, holding on my lap a tin box borrowed from Howard that morning – and that conversation I had before I could stop – in which I told him that I had met myself – my older self, Howard – I met her. Ridiculous I know – and him – no words, of course – how could he have words for what I said to him? – what could he say to this fucking madness? I pack the tin box with sausage rolls for me and Lisa, Lisa and me and walk across the disappearing city like she said and stepping over our past which covers this new city – to the bench – to our kingdom – our real city being built on this bench. The lake, the ducks uninteresting then and fingers holding the tin box tighter and head and eyes locked in the distance anticipating Lisa – Where is she? – I say that loud enough to hear in my voice this fear. And time buckles to be replaced by an uneven panicked heart – and before I can decide – I'm walking away from the bench – the sausage rolls left and most probably fed to those ducks – but me walking the steps Lisa would walk from her flat to me but not today – and standing beneath her window and calling then. Calling out and up to that third floor. Calling loud in a voice I don't recognise – a voice that scares me but still I call out. And there's people stopping and I say things like – my friend, I have to see my friend. Or my sister, to one of them I say – my sister, I have to see her. And holding back the words – I have to see myself – to add to the insanity already heard in my voice! Jesus Christ! And into the building and running up to the third floor and to Lisa's door – and there's someone watching. I'm calling out and hitting the door with my hand until it's sore. And more people then and neighbours worried. The door is opened and into Lisa's flat, in her bedroom and nothing. Nothing! No clothes – nothing of her – she's gone. I say it out loud. She's gone.

A pause.

Back in the home – back in the blue room and medication unswallowed – and Howard anxious now, unimportant him – because the past – our brief past has disappeared into the city – into the now and new. Before I held on to her voice – and to share with another what it was to be that alone – to sit back in the past and to be understood by Lisa. The past vanishes into the city and left alone back into the present where my head starts building a terrible truth. I hear myself saying into the blue room. These words. To live a life already

lived – to be bound by another and stolen of choice – to walk
what she has walked, to do what she has done. Again and
stronger. To live a life already lived – to be bound by another
and stolen of choice – to walk what she has walked, to do
what she has done. And what has she already made for me in
this new city – what moments and days and weeks has she
made – and people met – and where is the start and end of
me? And what is laid out invisibly – and might it run to a
dead woman's kitchen – and might there be another Lisa to
come and call on me? And what is she building right now
and where is she and why isn't she here to calm me? And the
past is burned – and fate is being made by her – destiny is
spun out – accident is killed – paths determined – life
unlived – undreamt – built – already built!

She screams. She stops.

A pause.

The dry days are over. And rain then. It's raining outside.

A light slowly fades down on THE OTHER LISA *– until she
disappears into the darkness.*

Only LISA *is lit now.*

A long pause.

*The quiet undulating sound of the wind and sea slowly
fades up.*

Then –

LISA. Time spins forward. And pulled away from all that life
I made.

Music.

Two cities both left now and a countryside then and not even
a town really, its name unimportant – but on a bit of a beach
and some houses – unevenly dotted and facing west.
(*Pause.*) And where's my younger self? Said loud that
question, so I could hear it come back to me in the wind.
Where is she? (*Pause.*) And will she learn to leave our past
behind her like I thought I had? Will time nearly fix her and

then lay out unafraid possibilities? (*Pause*.) How can she walk in this invisible track I'm making blindly. (*Pause, whispered*.) Never to return there. I can't. (*Pause*.) How do I go on living knowing I'm making a life for another? (*Pause*.) So a rope is thrown – and it passes over the journey I made to come to here – and into the city I left – and through the streets, it passes – and into that blue room surely locked – and to the young woman I once was – and into her hands that rope.

A pause.

We're bound.

A pause.

Lost and alive us two.

A pause.

Joined through time.

An aggressive change of light and THE OTHER LISA *visible again.*

The sound of their voices rewinding very fast.

It lasts thirty seconds and stops.

A moment of silence.

Blackout.

The End.

ENDA WALSH is a multi-award-winning Irish playwright. His work has been translated into over twenty languages and has been performed internationally since 1998.

His recent plays include *The Same* (2017), produced by Corcadorca; *Lazarus* (2016) with David Bowie at the New York Theater Workshop, *Arlington* (2016), *Ballyturk* (2014), *misterman* (2012) produced by Landmark Productions and the Galway International Arts Festival; and the operas *The First Child* (2021), *The Second Violinist* (2017), and *The Last Hotel* (2015), composed by Donnacha Dennehy and written and directed by Enda Walsh, and produced by Landmark Productions and the Irish National Opera.

His other plays include *The New Electric Ballroom*, *Penelope*, *The Walworth Farce*, *Chatroom*, *The Small Things*, *bedbound*, and *Disco Pigs*. He won a Tony Award for writing the book for the musical *Once*, which played on Broadway for three years and two years on the West End. Most recently Walsh wrote the book for the musical adaption of the 2016 film *Sing Street* by John Carney and scheduled for Broadway in the next year.

For over 10 years he has been supported by, and shown work at, St. Ann's Warehouse in Brooklyn. He has made an ongoing series of immersive theatre installations, *Rooms* with Paul Fahy, *Room 303*, *A Girl's Bedroom*, *Kitchen*, *Bathroom*, *Office 33A*, *Waiting Room*, *Changing Room*, and *Bedsit*.

His film work includes *Disco Pigs* (Temple Films/Renaissance) and *Hunger* (Blast/Film4).